Mummery

MUMMERY

Poems by

Maura Way

Press 53
Winston-Salem

Press 53, LLC
PO Box 30314
Winston-Salem, NC 27130

First Edition

Cover photo from pxhere.com, Public Domain

Author photo by VanderVeen Photographers
www.vanderveenphotographers.com

Cover design by Maura Way, Christopher Forrest,
and Kevin Morgan Watson

Library of Congress Control Number
2023945147

ISBN 978-1-950413-70-6

for Kram

Acknowledgments

The author thanks the editors of the publications where these poems first appeared, occasionally in different form:

100 Word Story, "Snowbird"
The Appalachian Review, "Fringes"
The Banyan Review, "Finally the Dogwood"
Barnstorm Journal, "Microburst"
Bedfellows, "Kid the Moon"
Bellevue Literary Review, "Cabbages and Kings"
Cease, Cows, "You Haven't Got the Sand"
Chapter House, "Salamander"
Cleaver Magazine, "March" & "Repartee"
Crack the Spine, "The Etymology of Dread"
Elevation Review, "Attention Fellow Schoolteachers:"
E-ratio Postmodern Poetry, "Creeping Morning Glory"
FEED, "Tao Once"
Folio, "Rising"
Hong Kong Review, "Mud Season"
Hotel Amerika, "Golden Surprise Fancy Club"
Landfill Journal, "Slow Cooker"
Northwest Cathexis Press, "Redecoration"
Opossum: a Literary Marsupial, "Dickensian" & "Remote Learning" (published as "Short Gods")
Plainsongs, "Boat Box Hot Spring"
Politics & Prose District Lines, "Sea Level"
The Red Ogre Review, "Iridium"
Schuylkill Valley Journal: Dispatches, "Washington's Sestina"
Yemassee, "Penumbra"

I am grateful to Trillium Arts for selecting and sponsoring me as an artist-in-residence. Thanks to New Garden Friends School for the time and support to go. Shout out to all the poets, but especially Karena Youtz, my first and best reader, Christopher Shipman for standing beside me (often literally), and Christopher Forrest for finding and then fostering this manuscript to fruition (the 4 f's). I appreciate Kevin Morgan Watson and everyone at Press 53 for making my second rodeo possible. —MW

Contents

Learning Management System

Patina

Since there's no hope of washing
it off, let's call it a day of mourning

for permanence, go ahead and feel
lonely for a minute. The advanced

oxidation of Liberty only makes
her more iconic. The water creates

the island. I am the rocky promontory
against which the surf pounds. I lull

churning seas to sleep, but I am only
a shallow dish, encrusted with a slow

moving sense of time. I am always over
flowing with imperfection and acid rain.

Gunne Sax

I got a pretty new
dress for my pussy

rejuvenation party.
Tiny pearl buttons

ran down the back.
I needed help with

closing them (and the
wrists). The lace was itchy.

You couldn't tell it
was hand-me-down.

Iridium

Confident folk write poems
about beavers and catalpa pods.
I want to notice the light. Gasping
for ecstasy, of me out of it, people
will catch up with me only after I
am charisma-drowned. Thin may
be worth it just for the outlandish
ensembles I could get away with.
Color can raise the dead. This is
my chunky bracelet, but it is a media
freak with no sense of history or
curiosity. My fibers cannot sit in
judgment. Another way out of it
is exaggeration which is making
me cry giant houndstooths. More
me, hurly-burly big. Still, machine-
made junk gnaws curiosity. You
can't have everything. Something
has to give. Sometimes it is you.

Remote Learning

Only the clicking remains, that same old
dog howling after his ambulance master.
If you hate yourself, you will only love
those with whom you have nothing
in common. Unless they hate you too,
then you'll have that. But the old-timey
kind of self-loathing has gone the way
of memorizing state capitals. Why bother
when you can always access the answers?
Relax. You can lose your embouchure all
you want now. Mute. Let the reeds dry out. We
have invented new instruments that you don't
even have to practice. I reverse-engineered the hole
in this flutophone. I will *make* the whole world sing.

Flue

The chimney pots are just your average robot couple. If they had arms, they could be intertwined. Their caps are the shiny stalwarts against a moving blue sky, low-tech, but after so many revolutions they are still made of the flimsy tin of ductwork over baked red clay. Robots don't even look like you anymore. They have become rounder and less avuncular. You extend the draft and guard against squirrel and elements in a way that is still based on terra cotta technology. We have forgotten that you serve us too. We cannot hear your ability to listen and respond to the untouchable weather. The venting is our own but will not save us or keep us warm. We don't even know what we have released.

"You Haven't Got the Sand"

was going to be a positive poem
but I already called it something
aggressive or self-loathing. There's
a cheer that spells aggressive; that's
positive. Lift me up and high knee me
deep inside a dolmen. Kill these woebegones
all the livelong day, bake me in a pie. Tell me
how to be. I feel farther and further away from
everyone and everything. That's why you get
a pet, that's why you go to bed early and pretend
not to hear the silence and premium channels,
sticking in your craw. I'm trying this new thing
where the less you know about people the better,
but I'm still tired of them and Lent is coming but
I'm not part of that anymore either. Once I went to
a Presidents' Day party and everyone dressed
like presidents. There were three Gerald Fords.
I was Geraldine Ferraro. I liked those people.
Don't ask questions or worse, cry like Pat
Schroeder. Draw a line. How can I be so
self-centered and lack ambition? Gritless. I
just want those fish tacos and to care about
cleaning up earlier than I do. The boundaries
get boring. I have bigger fish to fry if only
I could get this day-to-day down. I could stick
my head in a cool dark hole and pound.

Dickensian

I'm not pretty enough to
like trap music anymore.
Jacob Marley's chains are my
accompaniment. I forged them
link by link. Is learning really
making students suffer? They say
so, but ain't ignorance worse?
Not according to America. I didn't
want to *make* them learn. I like
assuming everyone wants to, deep
down, under the swag. This is a true
story: I don't want to anyone to feel
trapped in my classroom, hating the
unknown, yet wanting to be free.

Persuasion

The bar became a standing desk before my very eyes. I called the bullets *olives* because my points were for pacifists. A Mark Twain walked in and asked for a martini. He got me instead. He had nothing on Hal Holbrook. Claymation used to be more difficult. It's easy to get work done now. There is good news on the way; my job is to wait for it. *Comparison is the death of joy* but the beginning of market research, essays, and double-entry accounting which are some people's vocations. We argued with a Quakerly perseverance until hands turned past this happy hour. Take a little clay, throw it on the wheel. Fiddle the mental apparatus. *Make it a double.*

The Etymology of Dread

is highly unsatisfying. I suffer from
it. I have the world at my doorstep, but
I don't look forward to anything but nothing.
There is a hamster wheel I forgot to get
on, and now I'm hunkered down in the woodchips,
gnawing on a toilet paper roll. It keeps me busy. I
refuse to listen to advice, read even the most obvious
signs. This tank was designed to hold fish. I'm not
even crepuscular anymore. In a past life, I must have
eaten my young. I am at the mercy of large children.

Flexible Seating

The vice-principal found a
Francophile in the beanbag.
We call him Monsieur Frijole
to bolster his ego. Tiny chairs
gathered round but wouldn't
speak German, insisted that
they came from a child's
garden. So boisterously blue,
we couldn't block out their
cheer with our enormous
asses. All the other seating
options operated as traps.
Wire baskets never hold
books, attract rabbits, or
heal wounds. Come to tea
at my dream bureau; we will
float to the ceiling when we
laugh, but there's still space
to get our work done with
tennis balls stuck to our
untippable English chairs.

Attention Fellow Schoolteachers:

Always leave the year before you don't smile after October.
Arm yourself. This is not political. It is you who trained the
children to *run-hide-fight*. You who remained calm and packed
a classroom go-bag. We'll wear masks. Sure, you will curate rich
experiences and get paid for it. You will do an awful job and get
paid the same. Eventually, you will learn that you teach more
when you care less. Joy is in the wings, somewhat featherless but
proud—taking herself too seriously (like a doorjamb). No one will
ever say you are teaching civics well enough. *Think whatever you
want, I can too.* But I can't say it. There's nothing beautiful in the
dark. I don't know if I have another twenty years in me. It's so
late,   [remember   it can kill
You]
     and I'm still here: *cutting classes*
into quilts to be filled with golden
down   gagged, soggy, freezing my own ass off

Snowbird

The Latin teacher finally did retire. Her balcony now bends toward the sea. She is in a high-rise looking down at birds. Gulls scream and fly north to the next resort. All that's left now are pigeons on the patio. They scavenge through the purpling decorative cabbage. She hasn't seen a pelican yet, just the same birds she came here to get away from. They look like feathered cataracts in a kale eyeball. She sees a buried Titan with umbrella pectorals. It struggles to emerge from beneath the sodden November sand, beaten down by so many tenacious dog walkers. He has his eye on her.

Stanza

Slovenliness is all I have left of some
sort of fifth-degree anger. The raging
fuck it comes with rolls of fat and
pantomime Oh, it has enthusiasm,
but only for itself. Categories explode
and blossom into futureless moles.
I trollop through my own hasty
piles and slut's pennies. My work
always ends in heaps of hoggish
slatternly ways. I am overwhelmed
by objects and everything except
improvisation. I want to carve
out a space with nothing inside
for me to ruin. This sounds so
maudlin. I do manage to get to
the gynecologist, but never Spain.

The Mountain

Once my limbic
dumplings rise,
there's nothing
they can't do

crowned and radiant

I'll wear my union suit
with the gentle trap door

      (a wanton, an acorn)

and they'll all come out to meet me when I come

I'm an American
Songbag.

Prudence

Fourfold sadness descended
into my sense of humor. No
elixir could touch it. I waited

for machinas, but knew I would
have to write the programming
myself. A middle school is no

place for menopausal monsters
anymore. What is good is easy to
get, but so is enduring the terrible.

Tao

was once the hottest nightclub in Vegas. I
have been the valley for so long that my anger
has turned to sit-upons. The only water is
from capillary action. It defies gravity! When
you are a scar, you weren't built to forget
these things. You just can't erupt properly:
a hollow, a natural depression. My pillowy
rage is a laughable consolation. Cornflowers
nod to impenetrable rhythms. They aren't for
me. The dancing day becomes the meadow.

Redecoration

My objet d'art flagellates himself. I am not amused. My sous chef brooks no fools, obviously. My sense of belonging lags behind my collections. Even snow globes could overwhelm me. Your cut-outs annoy me because I am from the land of the cut-offs. Skin your knee in Pompeii and call it an accident. Flesh can be seen, the Latin teacher said. Dripping hollows fashion. Seeing Priapus requires a written waiver from your parents.

*

There's no place like my body. There's Montauk. I took a stone home with me. The lighthouse was open for self-guided tours. The rain turned into snow. I thought it would be different, same as when I look in a mirror. There are rouses all around us. The redcoats are inside out on the lawns of Leisurama. My body gets this; it dreams of Dick Cavett and goat cheese. I'm thinking about Amistad, of course. I'm thinking about the man who drove me to Montauk. I wrote him out of the story, but I'm willing to sit here and take questions, if you will applaud. I'm waiting for Stan Laurel to write me a letter.

*

Tricky baseball fathers will admit that I am right as rain. I usually notice assholes. The dull nobility of dicks wears me down. My epic expired on my way to another sandy ampersand. I will get home eventually.

Rule/Misrule

Washington's Sestina

for 1979

When I was six, I spotted a rat behind the radiator in my
classroom, but didn't say anything. George Washington loomed
over the class, unfinished, and glaring like a holy ghost or some
smoky saint. Raoul threw up every day because of the thermos of
milk his mom packed in his lunchbox. I looked away. I escaped
into chapter books with *Billy Jo Jive* and *Strawberry Girl.*

On the walk home one day, were piles of whole rooms, unfinished,
on the sidewalk near the high rises. Was it free? *No, chapter 8,
eviction,* my mom explained. *The bed belongs to another girl,*
pink canopy, ruffles, and all? Where will she sleep? *Jesus, Mary,
and Saint Joseph, just remember it is not up for grabs.* Men roll
an electric radiator, and a port-a-crib full of toys down the alley.
Landlord must have milked them dry.

Back home, a cartoon man jams on a junkyard radiator. Our
television set is enormous, but black and white. My unfinished
comic books are more colorful. I pour myself a glass of milk and
sit on the sofa that smells the least like cigarettes. There aren't girls
in most of these superhero stories. I like *Catwoman*; she's no saint,
but learns a lesson.

And on the news, a man from our local chapter says my dad will
strike soon because of some unfinished business. *Teachers aren't
just a bunch of sweet old ladies and milque-toast men!* My dad
teaches high school U.S. History, but he went to St. Anthony's. He
had nuns who would hold his fingers on the radiator to make him
be right-handed.

What am I going to do with a little girl? my dad told me he said
when I was born. Not repeat that chapter, I guess. They sent
me to school in a public demountable where girls don't have to
go to church, can wear pants, run for office, study radiation,
fix carburetors, sing *we could be engineers*. We are free to be
unfinished gems, win at soccer, not cross our Toughskins. We have
new saints: Harriet Tubman, disco, and peanut farmers. There are
chapters in our textbook the teachers said aren't true at all. The
milk of human reality, we're soaking in it. Parents with the Saint-
Exupéry philosophy want us to see rightly. Blizzards (like milk) are
always good for us. Make us stronger. Moms of other girls became
subs called *scabs*. School goes on without me.

The unfinished problems didn't disappear like our snowgirls in the
spring. Radiator rats remain. We get a new president, go back-to-
basics. My own chapters will melt and pond and spiral. A sweet
territory of marvelous spilt milk dribbles over the sharp edges.
Decades open and close, unfinished. Stateless songs strike broken
accordion metal, still radiating—

Sea Level

The ocean is a sonnet. I learned to
swim on Volta Place, took the 30 bus,
with my mom, down Wisconsin Avenue.
The ringing red cord is far above us:
I am glad my mother is here to reach
up. I have to ask adults on my way
to school. They never smile. *Back Door,* I screech.
Some days the driver doesn't stop. I sway
up front near powdery ladies, ask nicely
like a good girl. Car Wash. The Burger King.
Stop! Now late for school—to sit politely
out in echoing halls through class opening.
There are no routine tides or ascension:
Girls must stay buoyant and learn their lessons.

There is a Point in this Sump Pump

sesame seed bundt cake me laughs pushed from back ache up front
name is anger pop, tri-colored icy hot stain tongue make please,
stick out and see for real convinced not to be mad: dogs go mad
people get angry hey is for horses little pitchers have steel ears,
good little chopper with a shirt tucked in and not so easy now bad
girl stick is dead, not hanging three-foot on the nail pick me pick
me and the being is less satisfyingly so so

o) make something besides florets and they will love you more
o) and yes it is them but you care you care you atone
o) call a party no one wants to celebrate
o) say less you source
o) let down hymns

do what I say—stay in the shake: but you are saying to do it don't
hurry the digest: it feels better to be calm than red striped and
sucking oh I hate the rage the rage on me why be that way the bad
girl stick was a golden rule a sound quiet down! not good for your
insides to sizzle good at calming self and others like a saint (call me
that!) make nothing but no trouble and ahhh

So why not just take the licks and be a big Mac about it? that's the
way la la la la live for today you see it's meant to be pull off the
tab to reveal the free hot apple pie and the way the leaves blow in
the breeze and consolation comes again too easy and too early and
this is what I should be skinned for stop not

How can anyone know how I want to be treated anyway? But please don't tell me I'm supposed to be vocal about it or give me a bullshit job to do, Dr. Phil. You teach me how to treat you. So what if I give you my last french fry, the one I value most? Have you learned I am an easy mark or a good Samaritan?

Well, I would say that depends on if you're a motherfucker or not

I'm not your little ditto-sniffer
after all

Stand Up

The once upon
a time flattened
my muffet. I had
to learn not to tell
stories. It often feels
like having a mouth
full of steel wool. But
my stories don't make
any sense, require too
much explanation, and
no one believes them.
The purpose is usually
See how interesting I
am? or *Here's a topper:*
Best to just sit on crinoline
eating metal filament
swallowing punchlines

Single Panel

Anger is
excessive helpfulness and mischief.
Draw something under an umbrella,
naked with big eyes. Thighs over-
lapping genitalia. Now it is love.

First Flush

With the compulsion
to bloom, evergreen
camellias also fatten.
Voracious mouths
upon mouths want more,
cry out to upstage pert

berries, to defy even
the snow. There are days
to remember a desire to be
light and lithe. Once stuck
the answer is powerful
growth

however—another is to
stymie
flowering.
With strict pruning,
superior shoots
and hedges will form

Super Bowl

We never thought to
get nostalgic about
prudent coins, triple
strands of pearls, but
here we are. Available.
Our lines of scrimmage
may be marketing, which
used to disgust me. Velcro
hands across America uses a
protocol to develop empathy

for end users. I could be my
own offensive coordinator,
if I wanted to. All we have
left are our dollars. Holding.
Holding. There is a way to
prey on patriots. Houston,
we have problems. Upside
down upsets, owners of
New England (and Peggy):
crown thy good, open roofs.
The play clock keeps ticking.

Permanent Features

I fell asleep watching cartoons
and danced for the maypole. I
never learned about parallelism
or avoiding comma splices, but
I read novels and that sufficed. The
pole had Abraham Lincoln's face
on top but his hair was in a top
knot. The ribbons undulated
like highways as we braided
them. I have been a pole
worshipper since the courtesy
round, tutelary deities greased
with celestial fire. My village
will be fine. There's always
someone around who knows all the
rules, but forgets about the daffodils.

March

Sunlight sealed behind
cirrus behemoths, I am
deep in left field. Suited
up in stripes, I wait for
something to come my
way. One cloud becomes
a baobab tree. I'm grateful
for my hat. Leafless trees
are as cold and unforgiving
as bagged sandwiches. On
certain deserted islands,
there can't be enough space
for this kind of game. I pray
for lightning, any early victory.

Microburst

I remember 1989 too: in June a tree fell & another. I won an essay contest but couldn't get to my own award. One winner from every state (and me) got an all-expense-paid trip to Washington, DC. The hotel was in Virginia.

All the trees stayed up over there.

I don't think they believed that I couldn't get to the metro station because the power was out and cars were all smashed up in my neighborhood. I'm glad the winner from Hawaii got there. I don't think they invited Puerto Rico. I guess I was lucky they included me.

My essay was about the importance of sovereignty for the Baltic States. I was not the national winner.

Boat Box Hot Spring

Sail away in a sieve I tell
myself, tits deep in a barrel

lodged along the banks of
the Middle Fork. Some kind

April stars concur, plunge
into unseen Sawtooths. You

regulate the temperature with
the red buckets full of snow.

I don't mind the rotting smell.
I can't see the rusty bolts. I am

spinning and nude except
for a headlamp. The best

part of an adventure is not
knowing when you're on one.

Fringes

Patsy Cline courage
breaks the flower pot.

That's where I was
planted. With power

and certitude, I tried and
tried to flower. It worked.

We didn't know our own
strength until it caused

a decided destruction.
Now, speak my name.

La Paz

The piñata righted itself, all the sundries
neatly stay inside. Somehow this morning
I allow all the thoughts, and can watch them
float by in twisted waxy paper, call each one
by name. They aren't all sweet, but the nagging
negativity censor stays hoodwinked for once.
Cheery self-talk was not invited to this party.
Macadam-bound, my monkey mind approves
of me, is all my own. If I could keep this up,
I could have my thoughts and eat them too.
Stain my tongue purple and scamper free.

To Ambition:

Your restless nagging was all
for naughtiness. You made me
believe in promising meritocracies.
I rarely admitted you were part of me,
but all my failures are because of you.
You don't really want me anymore, but
I follow you like a stray desert dog, rut-
stuck, parading down abandoned main
streets. I bloomed where I was planted.
I went to seed. I gained the tenacity of
sagebrush but only to maintain a slim
survival. Ubiquitous improvisation isn't
everywhere: you wanted a bigger plan.
You keep telling me it is my fault because
I control everything. My terrible attitude
protects and then ruins each potential
hallelujah. If I can't accomplish anything,
why won't you let me just have a small
world to love? You go around in so
many circles, thirsty for popularity.
This canvass must end. I tried to shake
it out. I tried to use you for your motor,
but it ends up I knew more than your
mummery all along. My performance
is not obnoxious. My dizzy finishes
aren't yours. No one is clapping here.

Hunky Punk

I'm having all the classic
worries. In-vitro me back
to a time when anything
was possible. I could have
been a sycophant. Somehow
I managed to be assertive,
but not a go-getter. Faking
sick took chutzpah, sure,
but it was anxiety driven
and someone should have
called the authorities on me.
Now I have all the answers.
Never ever play hooky
from your own school
of buffoonery, Ma'am.

Mum's the Word

Mouthy

stay with me everything
    I waited for the sunrise special
and missed it   gaping baleless
bagels   null set   garbage
plate   banged pots and pans
at midnight   played taps silently
    resolved: my mouth will not be stopped
  don't need an extra rib to riff much
ado about my no thing
    I could be bene prolix let myself be
unaltered strangely short-listed semi-proud
bang bang comeday those guys
say anything   every scrap raff could
be the bull's eye   silence is mine enemy

Golden Surprise Fancy Club

The quixotic mummery gained
steam. I am always riding high
on the thigh. Quackery becomes
me. O Emmanuel, I have haughtily
paraded with so much more than
hubris. False pride braves on in
radical erasure. I am aware, at least
of that. Mask yourself royal. I'll
decide to guise for this cakewalk. . . .

Kid the Moon

Breathless boggarts appreciate
viewers like you when they
desiccate innocent Wednesdays
with the worst kind of gelatinous
thought. If *The Lawrence Welk
Show* still airs, why not believe
in a genius loci? I would talk to
the animals, fuck with your sugar
bowl. My horn of plenty overflows
with pancordian music. Champagne
ladies get along without me very
well. I'll follow this kelpie, fenwise
and worn, but she wants me pretty bad.

Pteridomania

Fiddlehead unfurled on top
of halibut estranged from
musical secondary school.
A cull of menu genre like my
foraging for fallopian slapstick.
Two lines, one line, straight
man, capped on a flat surface,
a fish-slapping dance for sure.

Delicately divide, fronds, upside
down, I will find the spore this
midsummer. My will o' the wisp
is a lantern under leather. It would
be so easy to get caught up in a
Victorian craze. Froggy went a
courtin' & so did I. I've got your
nose. That's the punchline.

Prolific

Nothing better to
do, other people.
The plutomaniacs
still bring a smile
to my face, as I
wander like a
proud and filthy
sasquatch. The
fertility doctors
are used to losers.
I'm a semi-finalist.

Mud Season

Winter plummets into wicker.
You could say spring would
stay under her thumb no
matter how much trash the
melting unearthed. I thought
the pear blossoms were a new
crust of snow. But, no, these
too-early flowers are here and
will die of their iron will. There
will be no lick of shade until
after the season fully shoulders
her responsibilities. Yes, I hear
that the bluebirds are back already,
but just looking at you under
the awningless veranda leaves
me blinded and cold.

Dirigible

inflated with
hydrogens I'm
      no moored
balloon (flammable)
helium is a better
suitor   inert and
expensive   creates lift
      so the old ladies
      can have babies
aerostat estrogen
direct me   it's fallow down
there romantic blimps have
already run their smooth
course better for marking
special occasions, the good
old years were supertoasted with
      unsteerable bubbles, whole
empires of unused masts

Boon Times

I am riddled with the worm moonlight.
One-ninth of my life was supposed to
be my childhood. First I grew up too
fast and then I extended the deadline.
Merlin told me not to, but I wouldn't
listen. For a time the adults complained
that the cat got my tongue. Now I do a
celebration dance if I manage to bite it.
My husband has noticed that my nose
has no face left to spite. Sometimes I
miss my rage. When the snow melts,
all the slime trails underneath become
visible. The robins go bananas. I want
to show off my fitness this eclipse. My
sluggish thaw hates her own chivalric
code, crocus heralds, and chemistry.

Cabbages and Kings

My sonogram is a grey goose.
My sonogram is Mona Lisa.
My sonogram is par for the course.
I saw the back of my father's head
and two-centimeter fibroids. There
was a raven in my sonogram and
dogwood petals flapping in the
wind. My sonogram is full of oysters.
I don't know how to read a sonogram.
My sonogram has an O. Henry ending.

The Bun House

Defiant cake-
      baking pagan
women hang
never-molding
     hot + buns up in
         Saxon rafters:
I have no sons,
only ha'pennies.
   My rub-a-dub
daughters, my
   wild panacea
        ceilings spell
certain home
coming soon signs.

Finally, the Dogwood

buds appear. Angry

green hearts of thorn

scream for attention.

Ugly duckling petals,

homely as artichoke,

bright contrast to wet

patchy wood. I used

to find this quiet rite

gleeful. Now I am so

tired of her tenacity.

Slow Cooker

I left my heart in the general
posole. I thought it would
be safe from harm. I got so
fat. Some pulling happened
while I thought about the crab's
immortality. I should be tender
by now. Silence is not peace: it is
the lack of courage in human meat.

Arabesque

There's research to support my
foot in your ass. Overarching
ogives from Idaho became
the only sky I knew. In these
cases mood became destiny.
In others you know you're
going to make it after all.
Philo T. Farnsworth shaped
life this way. The arc meets
the shank at zero angle. A knit
cap has no nose cone but can
still fly, at least according to
probability theory. At its most
countable, memory is also a
hyperbolic projectile. Image
dissectors animate the object.

Repartee

I've seen clowns from
both sides now. I've gone

far too long for a touch up.
Makeup! There is snow

down south and my roots
are showing. *Lipstick marks*

on the teeth are a sign of a
nervous breakdown, they

tell the young girls about
divorcees, in pantomime

and mummed tones. Screw
ball purification at once!

Lay it on thick. Busk them
blooming muses hither and

yon. Be a dear and pour
me a drink. Grace comes

in the morning; remarries in
Connecticut. What a hoot.

2000 Pieces

Turmoil is of uncertain origin: babysitters
club, hanging baskets, the wicker settee.
A Boisean telling me all about ginseng,
a British man scraping together bamboo.
Sloughing makes a complex broth which
cannot come undone. I'm a pliant twig
in the alchemy of ingredients. Always
work from the corners they say. Better to
solve a jigsaw puzzle in real time, while it's
happening to you. Tiramisu transmutes the
table scraps. Destroying one is gratifying too.

Salamander

You regrow limbs. I know what triggers
this kind of response. Cells remember. I
make a motherhood not by mitosis but re-
generation. A branch must break for the
dormant cytoplasm to even know we can
begin. Protect the wound. Foster magic in
your immune system; it will be how you find
the extent of your reach. It is only natural.
Just because it is in your genes, doesn't
mean it isn't difficult. They say you can
bend hell, they say you are a mudpuppy.
We know that scarring slows down your
process, but doesn't stop it. All together.

Penumbra

My father taught me a civil trick.
If you get caught during a rainstorm
at a downtown restaurant, just ask
the bartender if someone left a black
umbrella. They will present you with
a cardboard box chock full of them.
It is not a lie: someone really has left
behind each one. You have left many.
Part of the loophole is to make sure to
give that umbrella to someone who
needs it, or at the very least, leave it
in a shady vestibule, on the coat rack
next to that sad windbreaker. Otherwise
it doesn't count. Now they could call this
all a life hack, but I consider that lacking.
The process of inheritance is about so
much more than getting what you need.

Rising

I missed the sunrise
service. Amidst so
much sloughing and

gluttony, I'm still here.

I forgot my bonnet, my
tiny white Capezios, my

Winnie-the-Pooh dress,
but I am proud of what
I do remember.

Feasts move. The children

find the plastic egg encasing
my heart and immediately break

it open. I'll play

the bunny:
all the days are holy.

Creeping Morning Glory

She can't stay awake for the harbingers,
but still looks for them at dawn. Smooth
bringers, smoke signals, wisdom on the
half-shell: the clear-headed fingers of
five-year plans, next steps. She swiftly
falls into choice overload and retreats
into the moment as is so touted by TV
and books by people on TV. Then the
laughter-loving sleep, without finishing
the flow chart. Tomorrow will be the
same. She read articles about slowing
down; finds no advice on how to speed
up. Maybe this ox-eyed woman has the
secret? In deep sleep there is forgetting.
In this sofa there are coins. She will
not be a juggernaut on wheels. First
do no harm (*it's hard enough!*) and
then listen for the moonflowers.

Maura Way is the author of *Another Bungalow* (Press 53). Her poetry and flash memoir has been widely published in journals such as *The Appalachian Review*, *Poet Lore*, *Hong Kong Review*, *Puerto del Sol*, *Hotel Amerika*, and *The Potomac Review*. Her work has also been featured in the North Carolina Poetry Society's Poetry in Plain Sight program. Originally from Washington, DC, Maura lives in Greensboro, North Carolina, by way of Boise, Idaho. She has been an English teacher since 1995, most recently at New Garden Friends School.

www.ingramcontent.com/pod-product-compliance
Lightning Source LLC
Chambersburg PA
CBHW021515090426
42739CB00007B/617